NATIONAL GEOGRAPHIC

To the RESCUE

PATHFINDER EDITION

By Leslie Hall and Marissa Moss

CONTENTS

Fires

torm!

By Leslie Hall

Photographs by Mark Thiessen
National Geographic Photographer

A wildfire can destroy everything in its path. Find out how hotshot **firefighters** use science to battle fires on the ground and from the air.

Fighting Back. *In 2007, firefighters battled blazes throughout California.*

Clouds of smoke filled the sky. The day was as dark as night. A helicopter whirred overhead. Voices crackled commands over radios. Exploding propane tanks sounded like bombs. Scorching heat made it difficult for people to breathe.

That was the scene as firefighters battled huge blazes in California in 2007. Wildfires swept across San Diego County. The fires raced through forests and neighborhoods. They burned everything in their path.

The fires raged for days. They destroyed more than two billion dollars' worth of property. Nearly 2,000 families lost their homes.

What happened in California was dramatic. Yet wildfires are not unusual. Each year, some 100,000 wildfires blaze in the United States. They burn about two million hectares (five million acres) of land a year. Most wildfires occur in western states. That is where you find a deadly mix of drought, high temperatures, and lightning.

Fiery Factors

To understand wildfires, you need to know a few basic things about fire. A fire needs only three things. They are heat, fuel, and oxygen. This is what experts call the fire triangle.

Heat starts the fire and helps it burn. For a wildfire, the heat can be a sudden flash of lightning or heat from the sun. Even a blast of hot wind can cause fires.

Fuel is the stuff the fire burns. The fuel can be dry grass, fallen leaves, or dead bushes and trees. Oxygen is a gas in the air. It helps start the fire and keeps it blazing.

Wildfire is part of the natural life cycle of a forest. Just like a living creature, a forest can be healthy and growing. Or, it can be unhealthy and diseased. Wildfire can make helpful and important changes to a forest.

Helping Hands. *During the 2007 California wildfires, many people, such as this bystander, tried to rescue things from burning houses.*

Nature at Work

Small wildfires actually prevent larger and more destructive blazes. They burn dead brush and plants piled up on the forest floor. Removing this fuel makes it harder for larger fires to start.

Wildfires also set the stage for new life. When fire burns tree branches, sunlight can reach the ground. This gives new seedlings a chance to grow. Burned plants also add nutrients, or useful chemicals, to the soil.

Some trees don't just survive fire; they need it to thrive. Until the 1960s, the United States Forest Service tried to put out fires at the first spark. Then it was discovered that this was bad for a tree called the giant sequoia. The giant sequoia needs to be near high heat for its pinecones to release seeds. No fires meant no new giant sequoias.

A Growing Danger

If fire helps forests, why worry about it? The problem is most wildfires today are caused by people. Most often, people start fires due to carelessness. For example, sparks may spread from a campfire or even a burning cigarette. The result is more fires and more land destroyed than ever before.

Wildfires are a growing **danger** to people in the United States. Two changes have added to the **risk**. The first is that more people are moving closer to places that once were wilderness. So when a fire starts in a forest, people and homes are often nearby.

The second change is global warming. It is a worldwide rise in Earth's average temperature. Higher temperatures make spring and summer longer. That means less snow can fall in the winter. So there is less water from melting snow in the spring. These changes mean forests are drier longer. The drier a forest is, the more easily it burns. That's a recipe for more wildfires—and ones that burn longer.

Lost Homes. *Each year, wildfires destroy hundreds of homes. This house in California was burned in the wildfires of 2007.*

New Life. *When wildfires burn tree branches and shrubs, sunlight can reach the ground. This gives new plants a chance to grow.*

Into the Flames

Summer and fall are prime times for wildfires. That's no surprise. These seasons are hot and dry. In fact, people call this time of year the wildfire season.

During wildfire season, thousands of **brave** firefighters go to work in the woods. They risk their lives to battle blazes. The work is dangerous, but somehow irresistible.

National Geographic photographer Mark Thiessen knows that feeling. He started following fire in 1996 and hasn't stopped since. He spends his summers in a smoky haze. For instance, he photographed the San Diego fires for NATIONAL GEOGRAPHIC.

Thiessen has been right in the middle of firestorms. He says it can be very exciting. He says, "All your senses just come alive when you're in the middle of photographing fire."

Battling the Beast

Wildfires can race along at 14 kilometers (9 miles) an hour. Most people can't move that fast for long. Fire travels most rapidly uphill, especially if pushed along by wind.

Thiessen knows that a firefighter's job isn't to stop wildfires. That isn't possible. Instead, firefighters try to keep wildfires from spreading.

"Firefighters treat a wildfire like a fierce wild animal," Thiessen explains. "They attack it from the tail. That's the rear of the fire, where it started. Then they move up the flanks, or sides. The head is too dangerous to approach."

Just like a wild animal, a wildfire is unpredictable. You can't tell where it will go or what it will do. Rocketing sparks might start smaller fires in areas that seemed safe only seconds before. A sudden gust of wind might shoot fire in any direction.

Feeling the Heat. *Mark Thiessen has spent years photographing wildfires. He knows firsthand how dangerous they can be.*

Hotshot Heroes

Firefighters have different ways of fighting the flames. All the methods try to do the same thing. They take away a side of the fire triangle. Then the fire cannot burn and goes out.

Often, smokejumpers are the first line of attack against wildfires. They parachute out of planes into forest fires. They are called in when the land is too rugged to reach quickly on foot. If the fire still burns after 24 hours, other crews move in. Planes and helicopters may drop liquids on the fire to take away oxygen.

Firefighters often dig a fire line. It is a deep ditch at least a meter (3 feet) wide. The fire line clears away the fuel from both sides of the line. Another way to remove fuel is to start a backfire, or smaller blaze. It burns off fuel before the wildfire can. When the wildfire catches up, there is nothing left to burn.

Living With Fire

Although wildfires are part of a natural cycle, they have become human problems. So the U.S. government is working with firefighters and scientists to find the best ways to combat wildfires that affect people and communities.

Keeping people safe from wildfires isn't easy. It takes hard work. It takes **courage**. And it takes science.

Wordwise

brave: willing to do something that could hurt you

courage: not being afraid

danger: a situation where you could get hurt

firefighter: a person who fights a fire

risk: a situation where something bad could happen

Air Strike. *This plane is dropping special chemicals to slow a blaze.*

On the Line. *These brave firefighters put their lives on the line. They battle wildfires to keep people and property safe.*

Light

Lingesnes Lighthouse, Norway

house Lives

Lighthouse Lens. *Prisms in a Fresnel lens focus light into a single, powerful beam.*

By Marissa Moss

The wind howled and moaned. It was a cold, dark night in January 1856. The pounding waves crashed higher and higher, foaming against the tiny island off the coast of Maine. Through the spray, twin lighthouse beams pierced the night.

The keeper of the lighthouse wasn't home. He had left a few days earlier to get supplies. His wife and daughters were still on the island. They had to face the raging seas alone. As the seawater flooded into their home, Abbie wasted no time. She urged her mother and younger sisters to a higher, drier part of the island. Abbie stayed at the lighthouse station to face the storm. She was just 17 years old.

Why did she do it? Abbie knew someone had to keep the light shining through the dark night. Ships depended on it to guide them through the tossing seas and away from dangerous rocks. So Abbie braced herself against the wind and waves. She waded through the rushing waters to reach the lighthouse.

Abbie had no way of knowing that this was one of the biggest storms of the century. The rough seas continued to rage. Her father was not able to return to the island for four weeks. Night after night, Abbie tended the lighthouse. And not once did she let the light burn out.

Shining Bright

Sailors have depended on such warning lights for over two thousand years. Long ago, people burned fires along the shore to warn ships about underwater rocks or sharp coral reefs. The first lighthouse in the United States was built in Boston Harbor back in 1716.

Lighthouses also help sailors at sea know where they are. Many lighthouses send out a special pattern of flashing lights. By recognizing the different patterns, a ship's crew can tell which part of the coast it is near.

Before electricity, lighthouse keepers used whale oil or kerosene to light the tower's lamp. They placed a special glass lens around it. Augustin-Jean Fresnel created the lens in 1822. A Fresnel lens often has many sides, like a barrel. Each is made up of pieces of cut glass. They are called prisms. The prisms bend the lamp's light rays and focus them into a single, powerful beam. This brightens the light so much that sailors can see it from miles away.

Even so, skeletons of sunken ships litter coastlines around the U.S. They remind us of how dangerous sea travel can be. Yet countless other ships can thank the bright beams of light for leading them to safer waters. And their crews can thank people like Abbie for keeping those lights burning.

Leading Lady. *Ida Lewis was famous for the many rescues she made while working at Lime Rock Lighthouse (above). In 1869, a magazine put her picture on the cover (right).*

Risky Rescues

Fathers often passed on the job of lighthouse keeper to their sons. In several cases, the keeper's wife or daughter stepped in to fill the job. Ida Lewis is one of the best-known keepers. In 1854, her family moved to Lime Rock, Rhode Island. Soon after they got there, her father became ill. He could no longer climb the tower. So Ida took over.

She made the first of her many brave rescues in 1858. She was only 16. A small boat flipped over near the lighthouse. Ida sprang into action. She set off in her rowboat. She paddled through tall waves to reach the stranded sailors. One at a time, she pulled all four young men from the water safely into her boat.

Later, Ida rescued at least 14 more people. Stories of her bravery spread across the nation. Magazine articles described her rescues. People called Ida "the bravest woman in America." After her death, people gave the lighthouse a new name: Ida Lewis Rock Lighthouse.

Hard Living

Lighthouse keepers had to be more than brave. They also had to be tough. Towers usually stood in remote and harsh places. Some were on rocky points jutting into the ocean. Others were on windy cliffs or tiny islands. Weather in these places was wet and stormy.

Often, the only way to reach the closest town was by boat. Even simple things like getting to school or buying food were tough challenges.

A lighthouse keeper's duties were tough, too. The keeper had to climb the tower each evening to light the lamp. During the night, the keeper woke up many times to be sure the light was still burning. The keeper also scrubbed the lens and kept the windows clean. The lamp's soot could collect on the lens and dull the light.

At sunrise, the tired keeper trudged up the tower one last time to blow out the lamp. This process had to be repeated day in and day out, no matter the weather. Lives depended on keeping the light shining.

Living on the Edge

Life was especially tough at Point Bonita, in California. The lighthouse tower is on a narrow point at the entrance to San Francisco Bay. Along with the keeper's house, it clung to a wind-blown cliff high above the pounding water. The lighthouse was reached by an underground tunnel and a dangerous footpath. In the early 1900s, the Martin family lived at this remote place.

Sheer cliffs and rough water surrounded the Martins on all sides. Mrs. Martin worried about the safety of her young children. She tied long ropes to them when they played outside. This turned out to be a wise thing to do. One day, their daughter Dorothy slipped while playing. Mr. Martin found her hanging off the cliff, dangling by the rope! Soon after, the Martin family moved farther uphill.

Landslides and erosion destroyed the path to the lighthouse. In 1954, the Coast Guard built a suspension bridge stretching over the gully. Today, Point Bonita is the only U.S. lighthouse that you reach by crossing a suspension bridge.

A Thing of the Past

Point Bonita was the last lighthouse in California to need a keeper. As more and more places had electricity, lighthouses didn't need keepers. In fact, in 1886, the Statue of Liberty became the first lighthouse in the U.S. to use electricity. This famous American landmark served as a working lighthouse for 15 years!

Technology continued to improve. Machines and computers were invented that could turn lighthouses on and off automatically. Keepers and their families no longer had to live there.

Still, history remembers the brave families who led lighthouse lives. Thanks to their dedication and hard work, the rough seas were a bit safer, and sailors could count on a steady light to lead them home.

Guiding the Way. *Lighthouse towers are painted in different patterns, called daymarks. In daylight, the patterns helped sailors know what area they were sailing past.*

Cape Lookout, North Carolina

Assateague Island, Virginia

Tybee Island, Georgia

Save the Day

Find out how heroes save the day.
Then answer these questions.

1. What three things make up a fire triangle? How do they keep wildfires burning?
2. What details support the main idea that wildfires help forests?
3. Give examples of three ways that firefighters stop fires.
4. How did lighthouse keepers help sailors?
5. What is similar about firefighters and lighthouse keepers?